First Lessons®

Hammered Dulcimer

By Linda Thomas

Online Audio www.melbay.com/20066BCDEB

I0808781

AUDIO CONTENTS

1	Introduction	8	Children's Song of the Nativity	15	Silent Night - lesson
2	All Through the Night	9	Children's Song of the Nativity - lesson	16	St. Anne's Reel
3	All Through the Night - lesson	10	The Girl I Left Behind Me	17	St. Anne's Reel - lesson
4	The Ash Grove	11	The Girl I Left Behind Me - lesson	18	Sweet By And By
5	The Ash Grove - lesson	12	In The Garden	19	Sweet By And By - lesson
6	Away in a Manger	13	In The Garden - lesson	20	Sweet Hour Of Prayer
7	Away in a Manger - lesson	14	Silent Night	21	Sweet Hour Of Prayer - lesson

MEL BAY®

It doesn't get any easier.....

1 2 3 4 5 6 7 8 9 0

Visit us on the Web at www.melbay.com — E-mail us at email@melbay.com

Contents

Introduction 3

Acknowledgments 4

About the Hammered Dulcimer 5

Tips For Playing the Tunes 6

Hammered Dulcimer Tuning Chart 7

Notation Symbols 8

Notes/Symbols/Techniques/Theory 9

Songs

All Through the Night *10*

The Ash Grove *12*

Away in a Manger *14*

Children's Song of the Nativity *16*

The Girl I Left Behind Me *18*

In the Garden *19*

Silent Night *22*

St. Anne's Reel *24*

Sweet By and By *25*

Sweet Hour Of Prayer *28*

Linda Thomas's Discography 30

Listening/Instructional Materials 30

About the Author 31

Performances 32

Introduction

First Lessons Hammered Dulcimer is designed to instruct beginning players on the instrument. The collection of melodies, written in standard notation, include hymns, holiday music, folk songs and fiddle tunes; also included are lyrics and suggested chords for accompanying instruments. The accompanying CD offers two tracks for each selection to include:

1) performance track with rhythm guitar

2) instructional track with detailed phrase-by-phrase demonstration

The guided audio instruction, at a slower tempo, will also provide invaluable for the "by ear" player. Also, remember to "play along" with the performance track to build your speed and maintain a steady beat for each song!

Please feel free to contact me with any specific questions you may have. Good luck with your playing and have fun with your hammered dulcimer.

Linda G. Thomas
lindadan@primary.net
(816) 763-5040

Linda G. Thomas

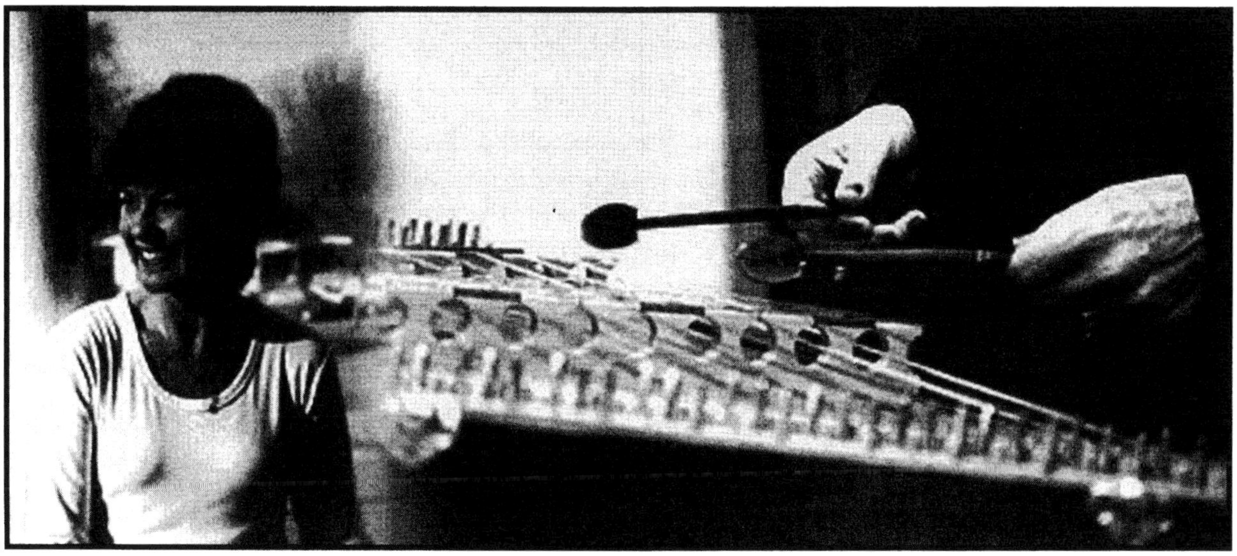

Acknowledgments

I would like to thank Bill Bay and Mel Bay Publications for helping people around the world realize their dreams to play an instrument; also, a special thanks for including my arrangements for hammered dulcimer in this series.

A special thank you to Dan DeLancey for his invaluable recording work on this project. And, a special thank you to Steve Kaufman for his encouragement through the years.

Hammered Dulcimer:	Linda G. Thomas
Rhythm Guitar:	Dan DeLancey
Photography:	Annie Tichenor Ted Haub Scott Jackson
Correspondence:	Linda G. Thomas lindadan@primary.net (816) 763-5040

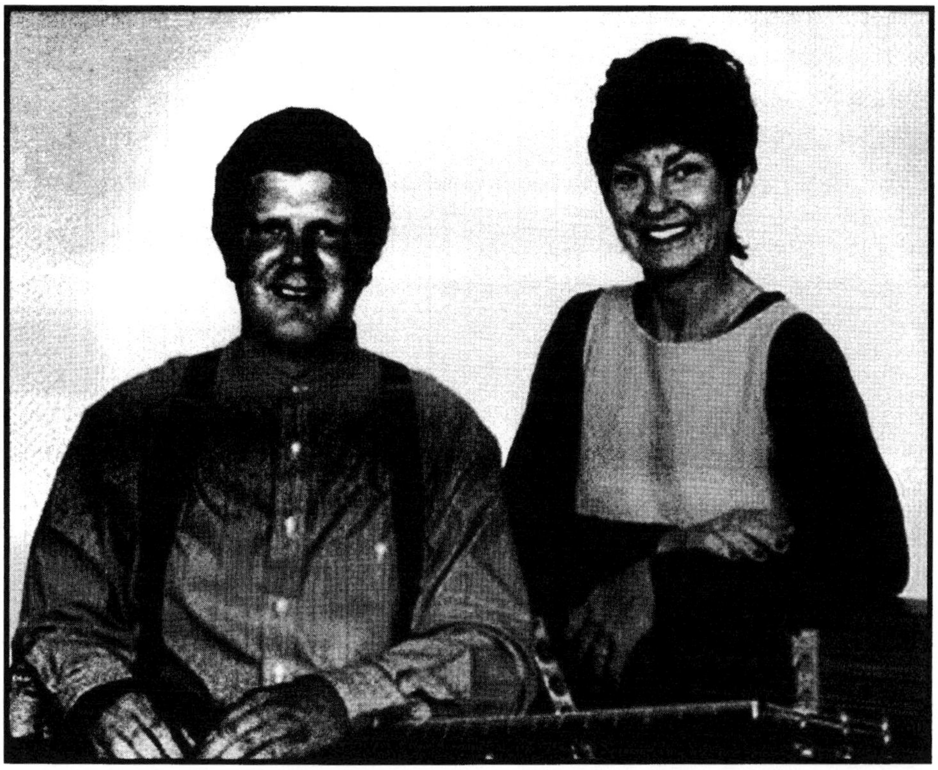

Dan Delancey and Linda G. Thomas

About the Hammered Dulcimer

The hammered dulcimer is a trapezoid shaped instrument with tightly stretched metal strings that are plucked or struck with hammers or mallets. The dulcimer is said to have originated in the Middle East and was brought to America from Europe by the colonists. The dulcimer is a very versatile instrument and is equally popular among classical, folk, and traditional players.

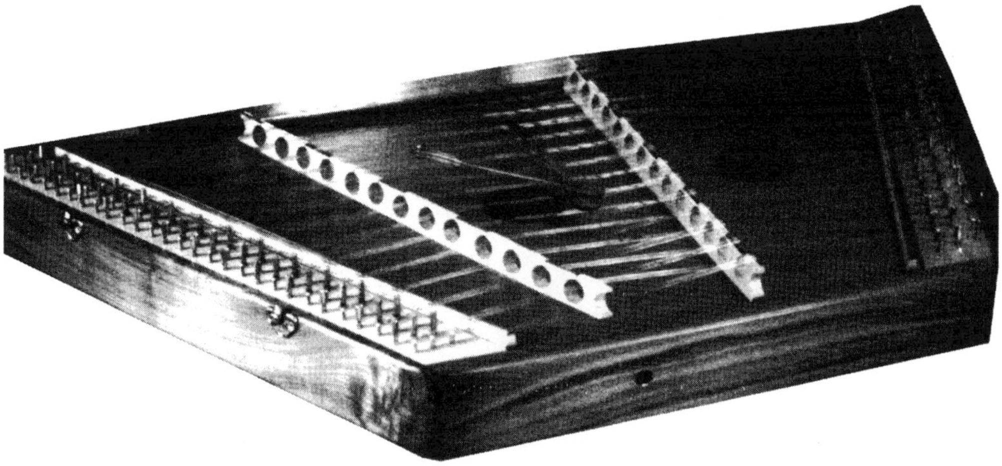

"The Baby Grand" by David Lindsey

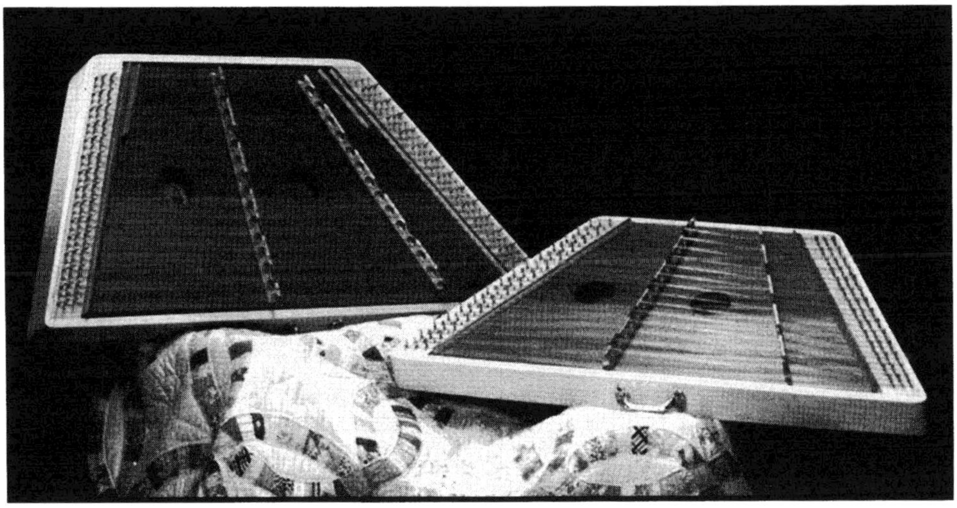

"The Grand" and "The Baby Grand" by David Lindsey

Tips For Playing the Tunes

All Through the Night — Phrases 1, 2, and 4 in this piece all have the same rhythmic pattern; be sure to hold the dotted quarter note 1 1/2 beats. Also, notice the dotted half note at the end of each of those phrases which receives 3 beats. The quarter rest at the end of those phrases will not be "silent" as the strings on the dulcimer will continue to ring but that rest does allow for a natural place for a singer to take a breath. Phrase 3 is a steady beat of quarter notes — be careful not to rush the tempo here.

The Ash Grove — This song is made up of several sequences — a pattern that is repeated over and over at a higher or lower pitch; notice that the same pattern played in measures 3 and 4 is repeated in measures 5 and 6 but it is played 1 step lower. There is also a sequence of notes from measures 17 and 18 to measures 19 and 20 and measures 21 and 22, each time moving down one step lower. Training your ear to listen for repeated or similar patterns will also help your playing in other songs!

Away in a Manger — Each phrase in this song uses the same rhythm pattern so that will help you learn the tune more quickly. You will notice that the song begins with a "pick-up" note (1 beat taken from the last measure in the song) so you will start playing on beat 3 of the count. Count carefully to give the half note 2 beats at the end of each phrase.

Children's Song of the Nativity — This song starts with 4 eighth notes, so be very careful to count carefully! This same pattern is repeated again in phrases 2 and 4, so working out that pattern will make learning the rest of the song more fun. Alternate hands (R-L-R-L) to give the pattern a smooth sound and help you achieve more speed.

The Girl I Left Behind Me — Much of this song is scale-wise patterns; however, watch out for the endings of the phrases—measures 6, 7, and 8 and 14, 15, and 16. These endings are intervals of thirds (every other course) so work through these places carefully. Try learning this tune in 2 measure segments, then adding 2 segments together; this will also help you memorize the tune as you learn it! Remember to alternate hands (R-L-R-L) to give your playing a smooth sound and to help you achieve speed!

In the Garden — You can be very "free" with the tempo of this song and play it with a great deal of feeling; at some time you may even experiment with a rubato interpretation. This will allow you to speed up and slow down for a more flexible feeling rather than a rigid steady beat. Try to "sing the song" in your mind as you play and that feeling will come through in your playing!

Silent Night — Remember to alternate hands when you play this song. The slow tempo of the song makes it easy to reach all the notes with one hand; however, your playing will sound much smoother if you use both hands. Also, try to "see" the patterns on your instrument - this is a song that you'll want to perform for an audience as soon as possible!

St. Anne's Reel — Remember to start slowly with this tune– speed will come with time. The following hand patterns will help you through the patterns:

Measures 1 and 5: R-R-L-R-L-R-L
Measures 6 and 7: R-L-R-R-L-R-R

Watch out for the passage in measures 11 and 12—you will skip notes to play every other course marker on this pattern. Good Luck on this one—it will soon become one of your favorites, I'm sure!

Sweet By and By— This song is made up of mostly scale-wise patterns with repeated rhythm patterns throughout. You can experiment with the tempo after you learn the song—I like a "gospel" sound! Sing the melody in your mind as you play this song and enjoy!

Sweet Hour of Prayer — Remember to play across the bridge on this song; the A-B-C♯-D in measures 3 and 4 are on the left side of the treble bridge. Although A and B are also on the right side of the bridge, to play them on the left side makes them in a smoother line with the C♯. Again, try to alternate hands for a smoother sound.

Tuning Chart for 15/14 Hammered Dulcimer

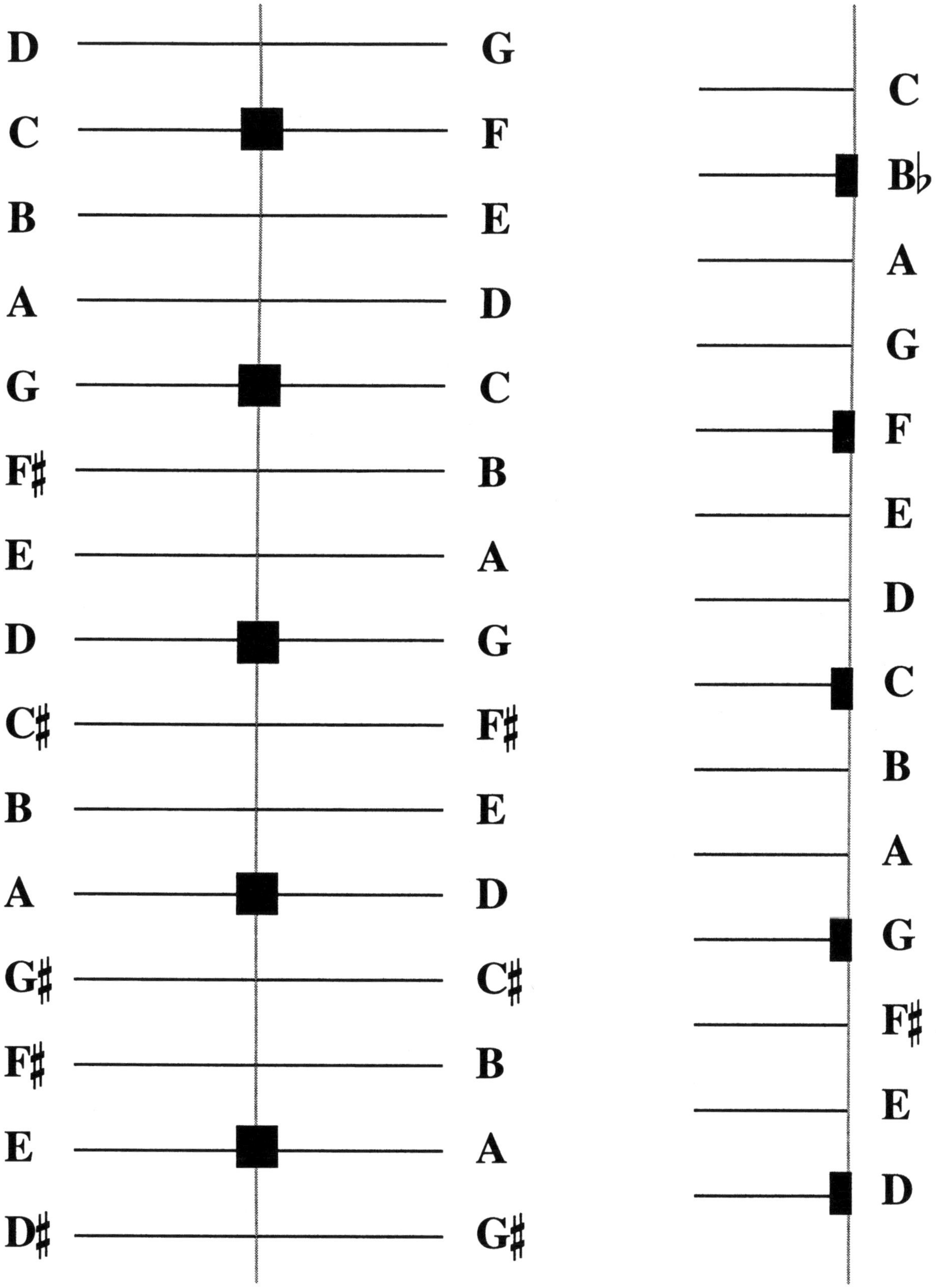

Notation Symbols

Circled numbers refer to the key on the next page.

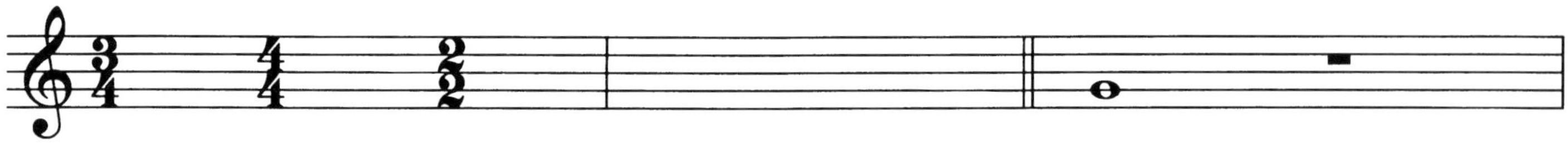

① **Time Signatures (or)**
Meter Signatures

② **Measures**
Bar Lines
Double Bar Lines

③ **Whole Note**
Whole Rest

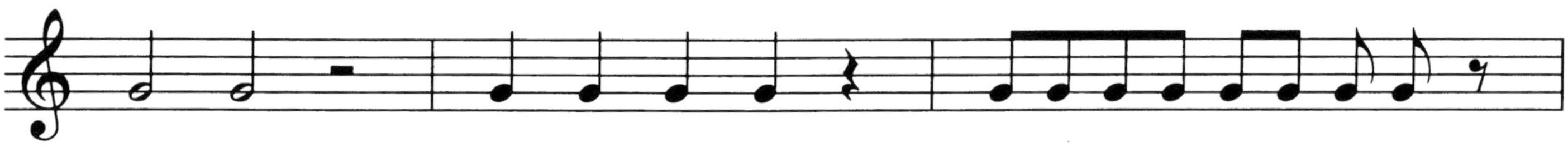

④ **Half Notes**
Half Rest

⑤ **Quarter Notes**
Quarter Rest

⑥ **Eighth Notes**
Eighth Rest

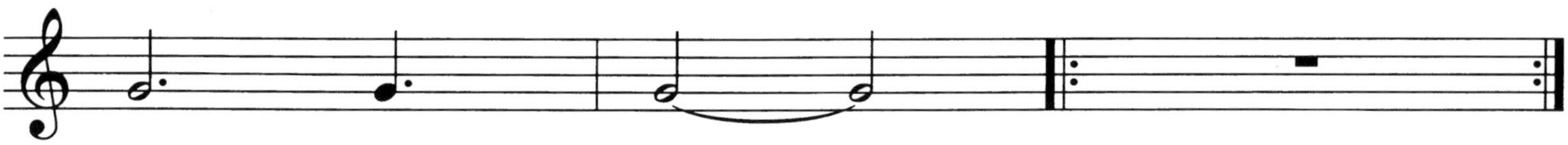

⑦ **Dotted Half Note**
Dotted Quarter Note

⑧ **Tied Notes**

⑨ **Repeat Signs**

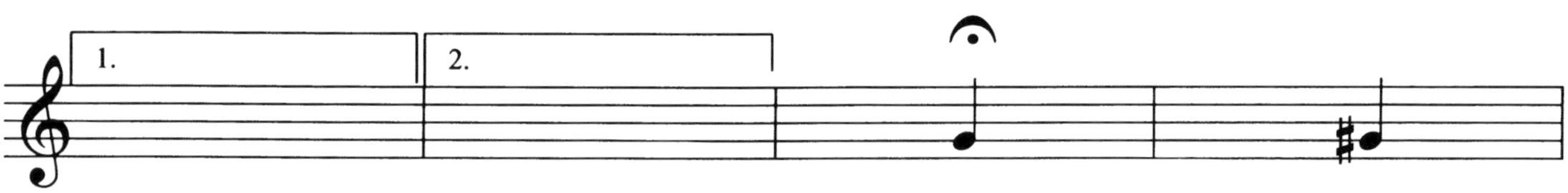

⑩ **1st and 2nd Endings**

⑪ **Fermata**

⑫ **Sharp/Accidental**

Notes / Symbols / Techniques / Theory

The following examples, all shown using the note G, are representative of the notation used in this book.

① **Time or Meter Signature** – The top number of the time signature represents the number of beats in each measure or set; the bottom number represents the type of note that gets one beat.

② **Measure** – A measure of music is a means of dividing the notes into equal sets of beats; the measures (sets of beats) are divided by vertical lines called bar lines. A double bar line shows the end of the song.

③ **Whole Note/Rest** – The whole note represents the longest value of any of the individual notes. A whole rest is a period of silence of the same value.

④ **Half Note/Rest** – The half note represents half the amount of time that a whole note gets; for example, if a whole note gets 4 beats (as in 4/4 time) the half note would get 2 beats. A half rest is a period of silence of the same value.

⑤ **Quarter Note/Rest** – The quarter note represents a quarter of the amount of time that a whole note gets; for example if a whole note gets 4 beats the quarter note would get 1 beat. A quarter rest is a period of silence of the same value.

⑥ **Eighth Note/Rest** – The eighth note represents an eighth of the amount of time that a whole note gets; for example, a whole note gets 4 beats the eighth note would get 1/2 beat. Eighth notes may be written with a "flag" at the top or joined together in groups by a bar at the top. An eighth rest is a period of silence of the same value.

⑦ **Dotted Notes** – A dot beside a note increases the value of the note by 1/2 of the original value; for example, if the half note gets 2 beats, the dotted half would get 3 beats. Or, if a quarter note gets 1 beat, the dotted quarter would get 1 1/2 beats.

⑧ **Tied Notes** – When 2 identical notes (both are the same pitch) are tied together the values of the 2 notes are added together. The note is held for the total value, not re-struck.

⑨ **Repeat Signs** – A double bar line with 2 dots means repeat; a repeat sign at the end of a section means repeat back to the beginning. Or, if 2 repeat signs face each other, you will repeat the measures between the 2 repeats.

⑩ **1st and 2nd Endings** – A numbered bracket above the ending notes in a section indicates a difference in notation when the section is repeated; the notation under bracket 1 is played the first time through; at the end of the second time through, the notes under bracket 2 are played (skipping over the notes under bracket 1).

⑪ **Fermata** – A fermata placed above a note indicates a hold; the tempo is broken to hold that note a longer period of time.

⑫ **Sharp/Accidental** – A sharp placed in front of a note (that is not included in the Key Signature at the beginning) is called an accidental and means to play that one particular note a half step higher; the accidental remains in effect throughout a measure.

All Through the Night

Key: G Major
Meter: Sets of 4

Traditional Welsh Folk Song
Arranged by L.G.T.

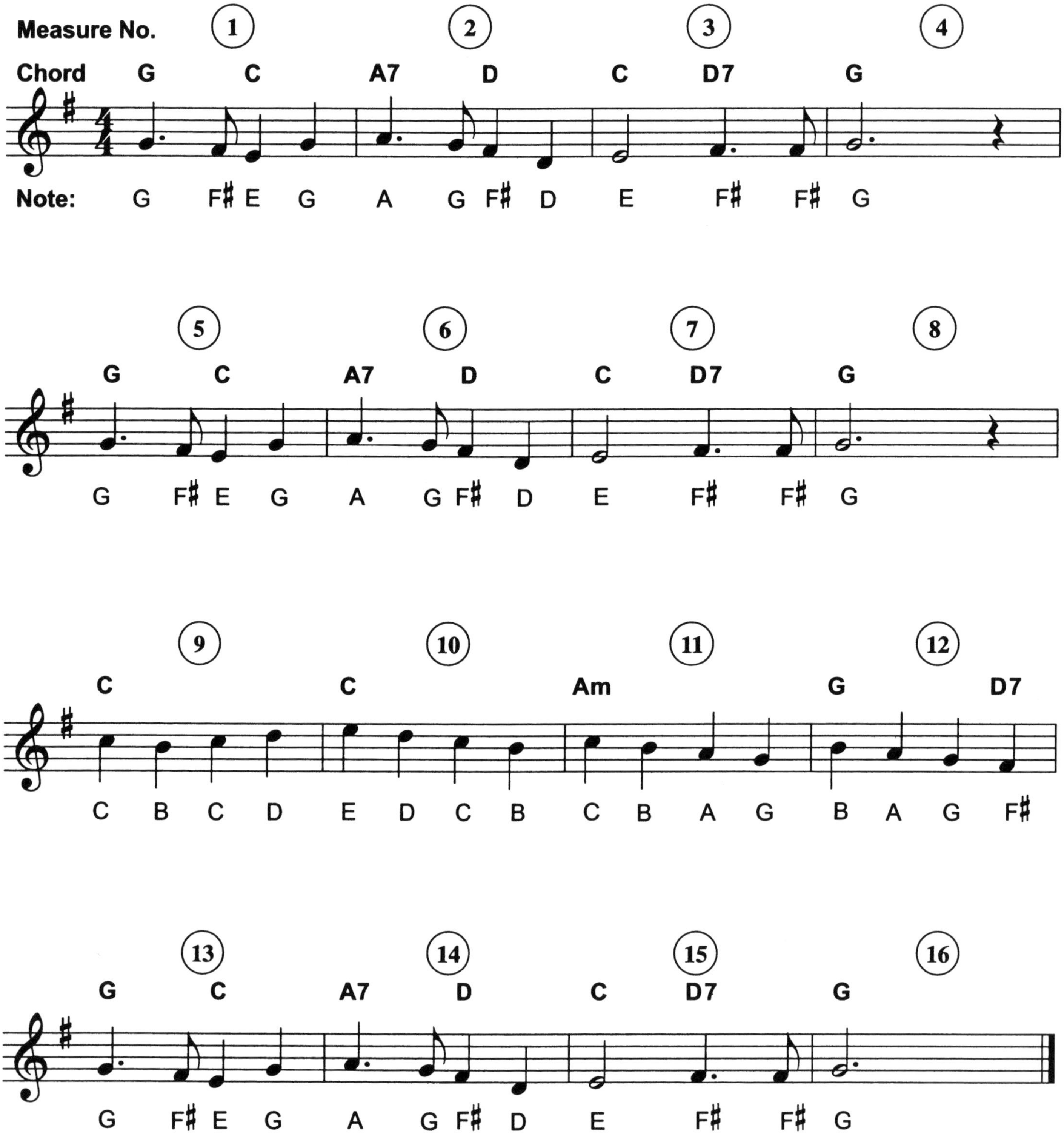

All Through the Night

1 Sleep, my child, and peace attend thee all thro' the night;
Guardian angels God will send thee all thro' the night;
Soft the drowsy hours are creeping, Hill and vale in slumber steeping;
Mother, here, her watch is keeping all thro' the night.

2 While the moon her watch is keeping all thro' the night,
While the weary world is sleeping all thro' the night.
O'er thy spirit gently stealing, Visions of delight revealing,
Breathes a pure and holy feeling all thro' the night.

The Ash Grove

Key: G Major
Meter: Sets of 3

Traditional Welsh Folk Song
Arranged by L.G.T.

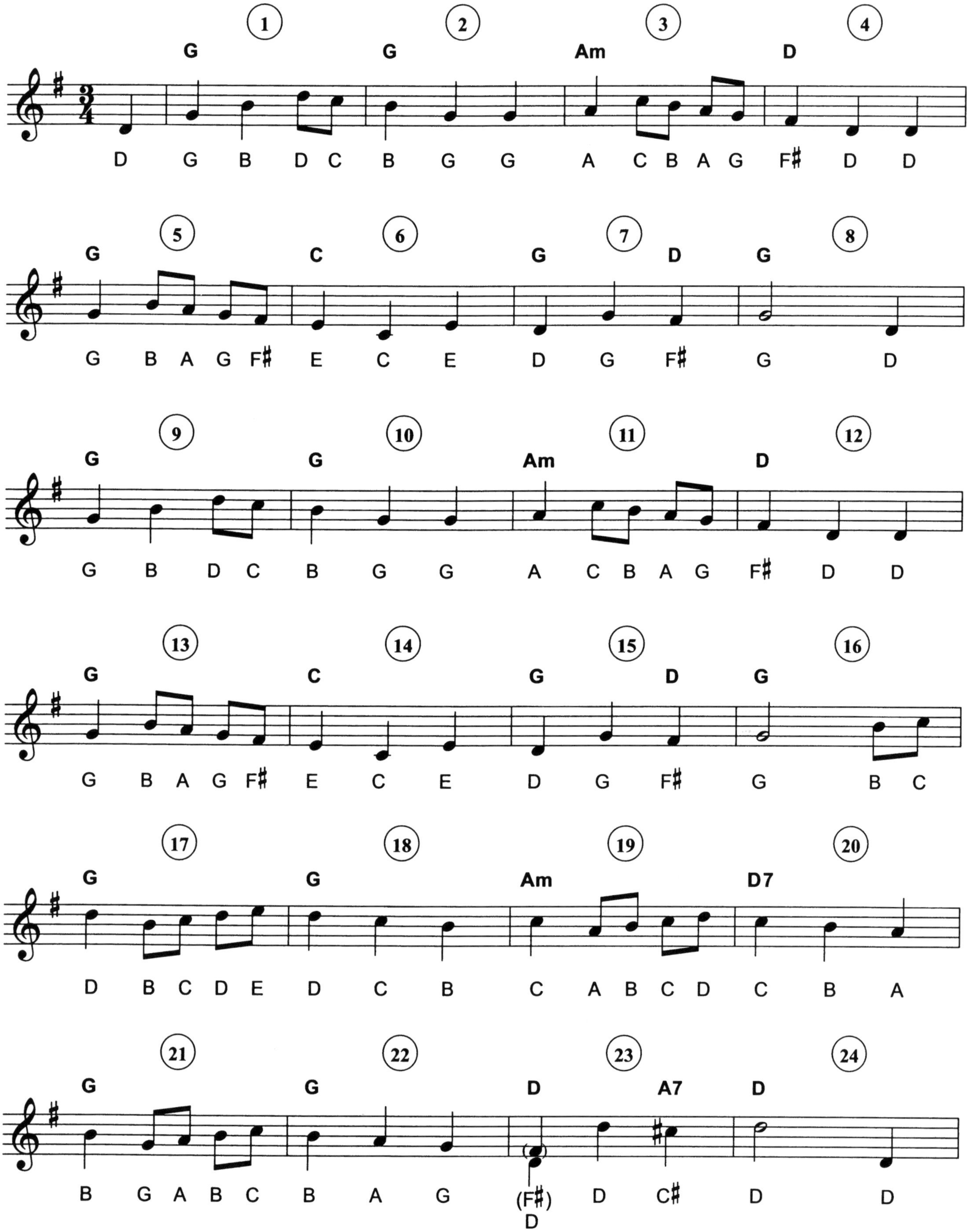

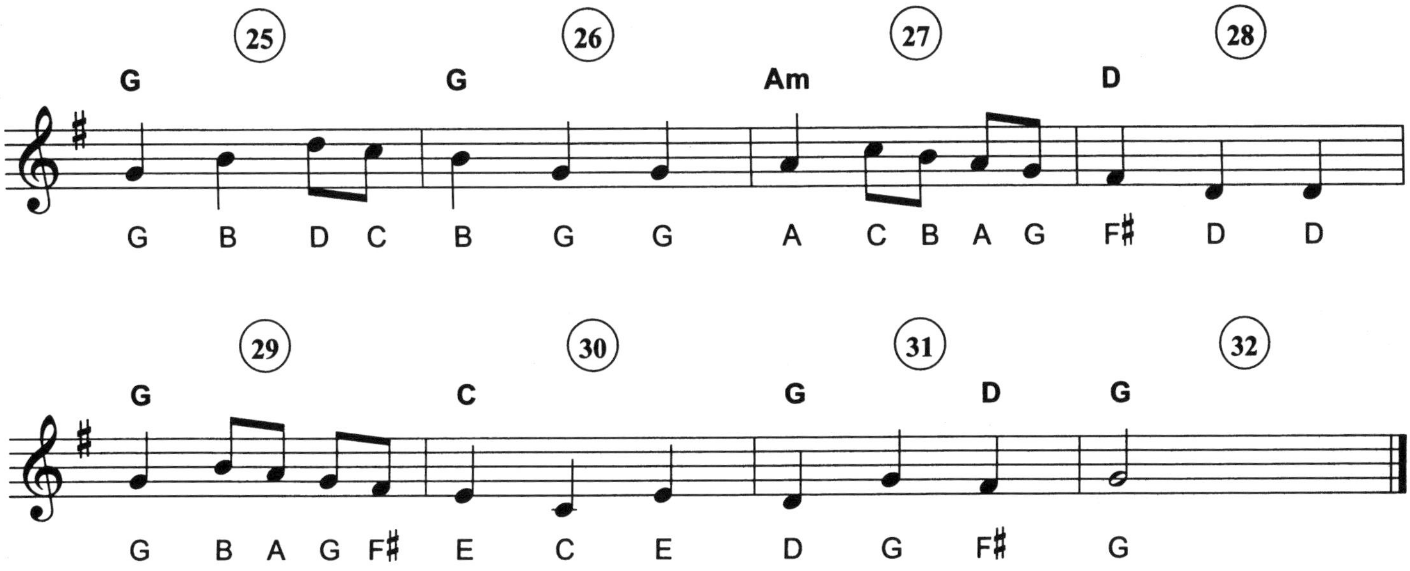

The Ash Grove

1 Down yonder green valley where streamlets meander,
When twilight is fading I pensively rove,
Or at the bright noontide in solitude wander
Amid the dark shades of the lonely ash grove.

'Tis there where the blackbird is cheerfully singing,
Each warbler enchants with his note from the tree.
Ah, then little think I of sorrow or sadness;
The ash grove enchanting spells beauty for me.

2 The ash grove, how graceful, how plainly 'tis speaking,
The harp through it playing has language for me;
Whenever the light through its branches is breaking,
A host of kind faces is gazing on me;

The friends of my childhood again are before me,
Each step wakes a mem'ry as freely I roam;
With soft whispers laden, its leaves rustle o'er me,
The ash grove, the ash grove alone is my home.

Away in a Manger

Key: G Major
Meter: Sets of 3

Traditional German Carol
Arranged by L.G.T.

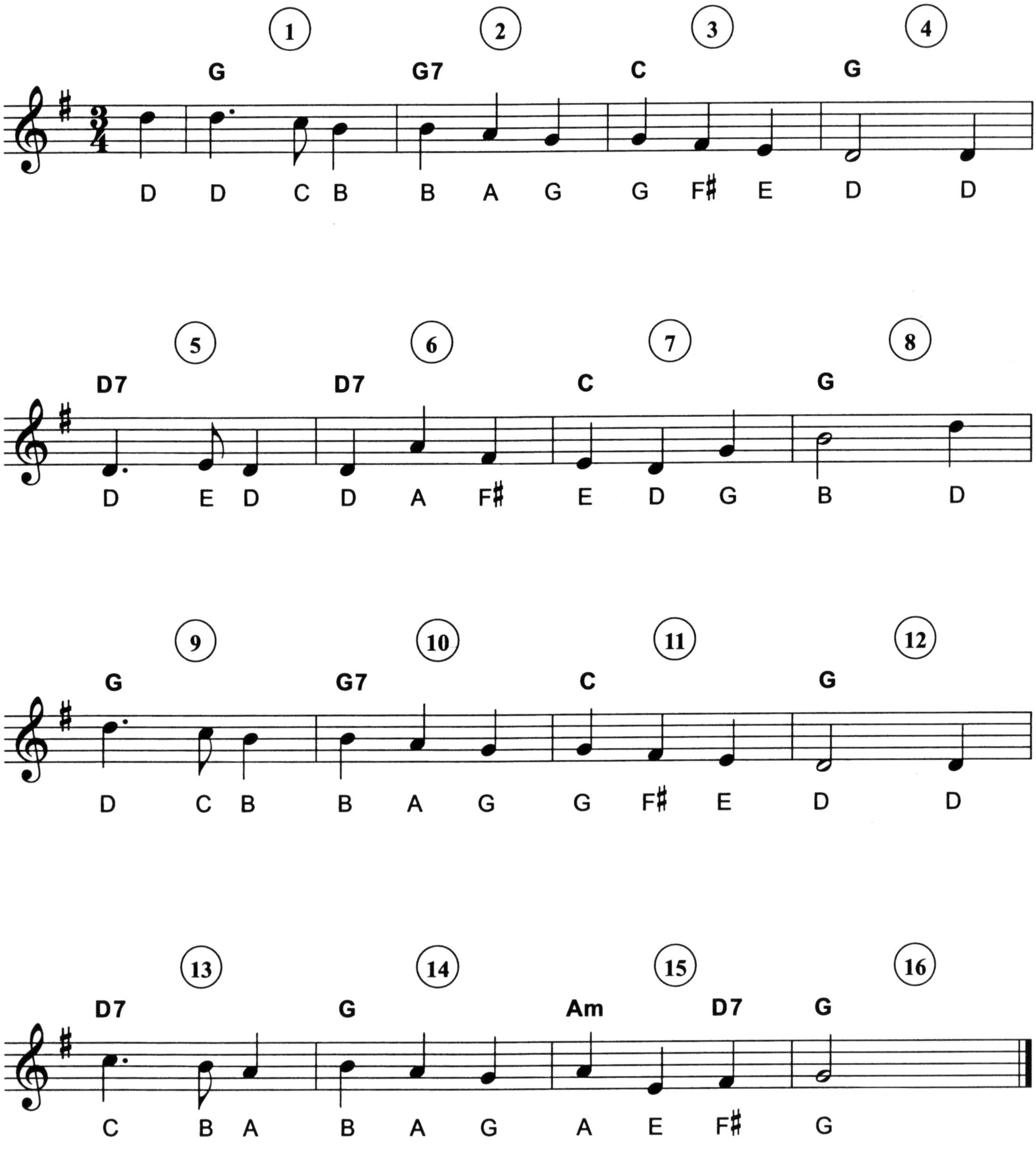

Away in a Manger

1 Away in a manger, no crib for His bed
The little Lord Jesus laid down His sweet head.
The stars in the sky looked down where He lay,
The little Lord Jesus, asleep on the hay.

2 The cattle are lowing, the Baby awakes,
But little Lord Jesus, no crying He makes.
I love Thee, Lord Jesus, look down from the sky,
And stay by my cradle 'til morning is nigh.

3 Be near me, Lord Jesus, I ask Thee to stay
Close by me forever, and love me, I pray.
Bless all the dear children in thy tender care,
And fit us for heaven to live with Thee there.

Children's Song of the Nativity

Key: G Major
Meter: Sets of 3

Traditional English Carol
Arranged by L.G.T.

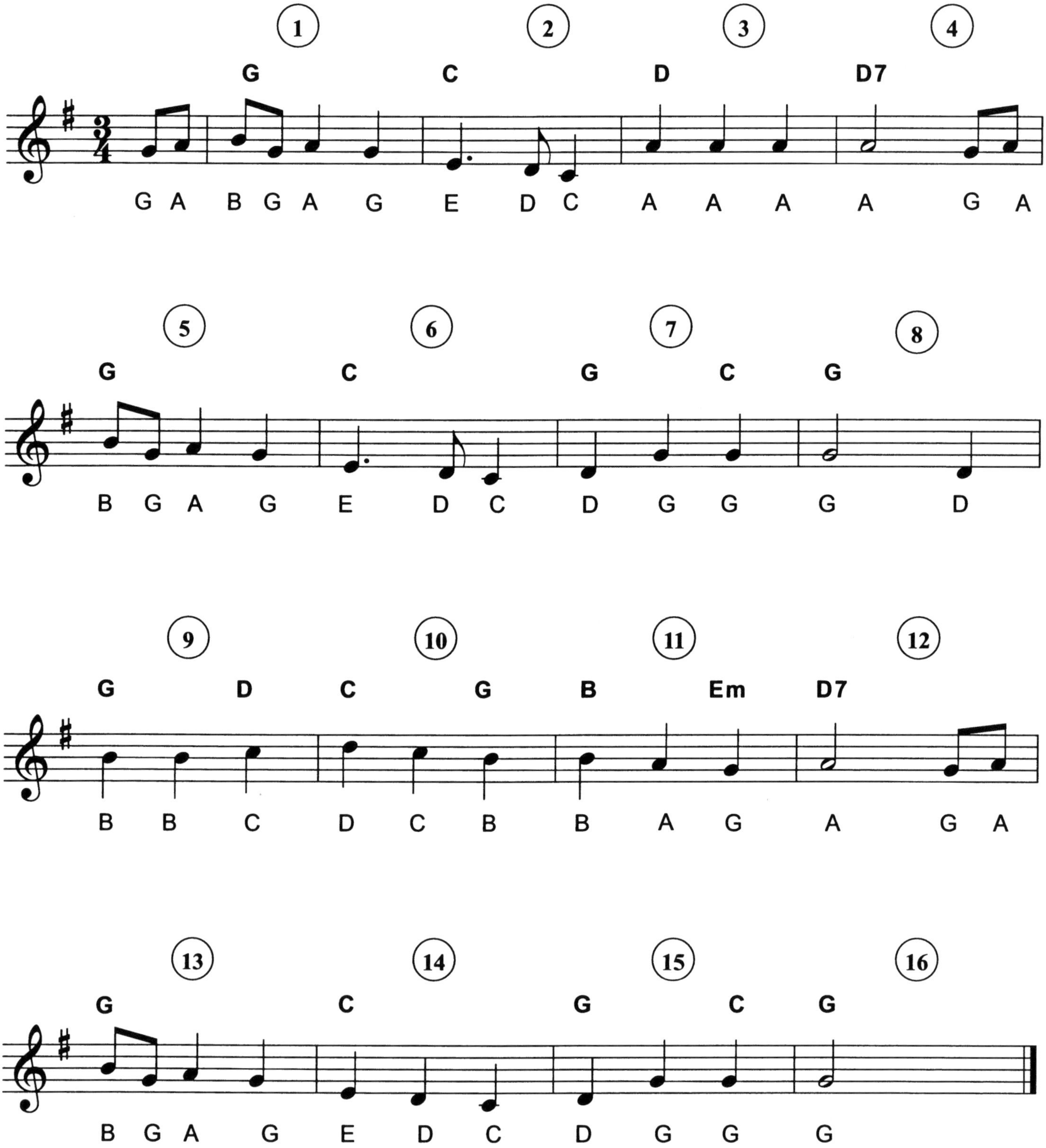

Children's Song of the Nativity

1 How far is it to Bethlehem? Not very far.
Shall we find the stable room Lit by a star?

2 Can we see the little child, Is He within?
If we lift the wooden latch May we go in?

3 May we stroke the creatures there, Ox, ass, or sheep?
May we peep like them and see Jesus asleep?

4 If we touch His tiny hand Will He awake?
Will He know we've come so far Just for His sake?

5 Great kings have precious gifts, And we have naught,
Little smiles and little tears Are all we brought.

6 For all weary children Mary must weep.
Here, on His bed of straw Sleep, children, sleep.

7 God in His mother's arms, Babes in the byre,
Sleep, as they sleep who find Their heart's desire.

The Girl I Left Behind Me

Key: G Major
Meter: Sets of 2

Traditional
Arranged by L.G.T.

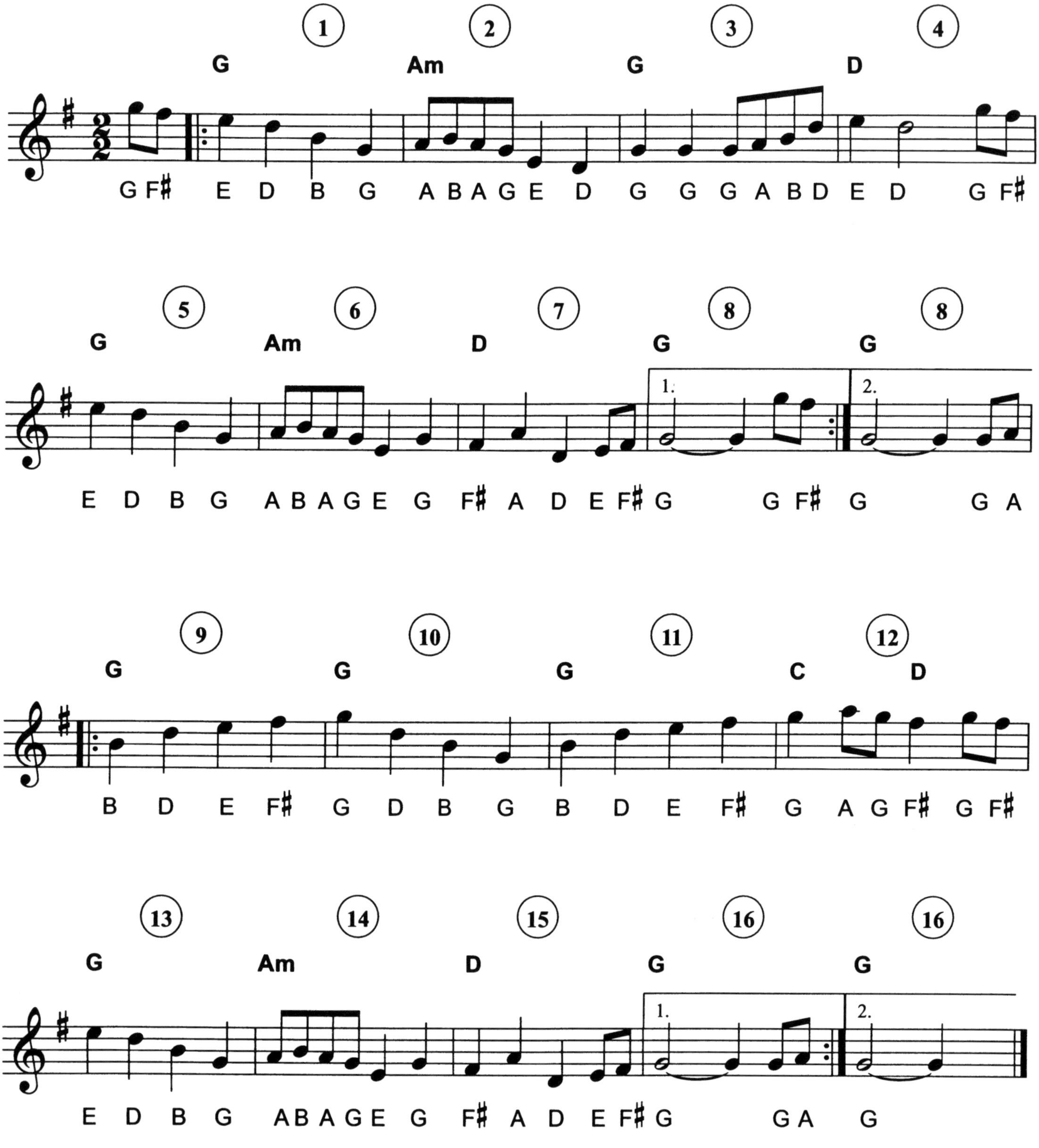

In the Garden

Key: G Major
Meter: Sets of 3

C. Austin Miles
Arranged by L.G.T.

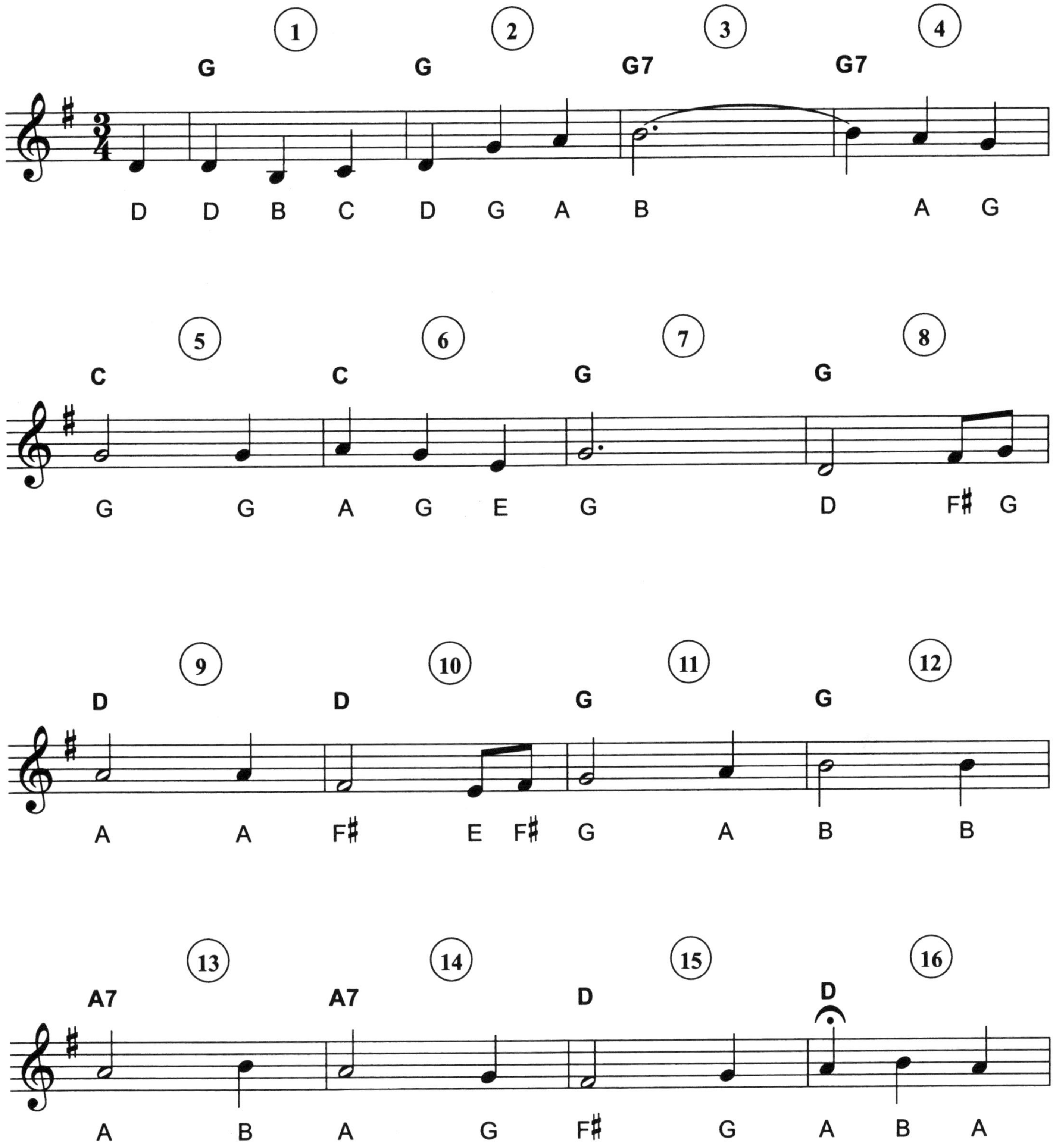

Continue

In the Garden (cont.)

CHORUS

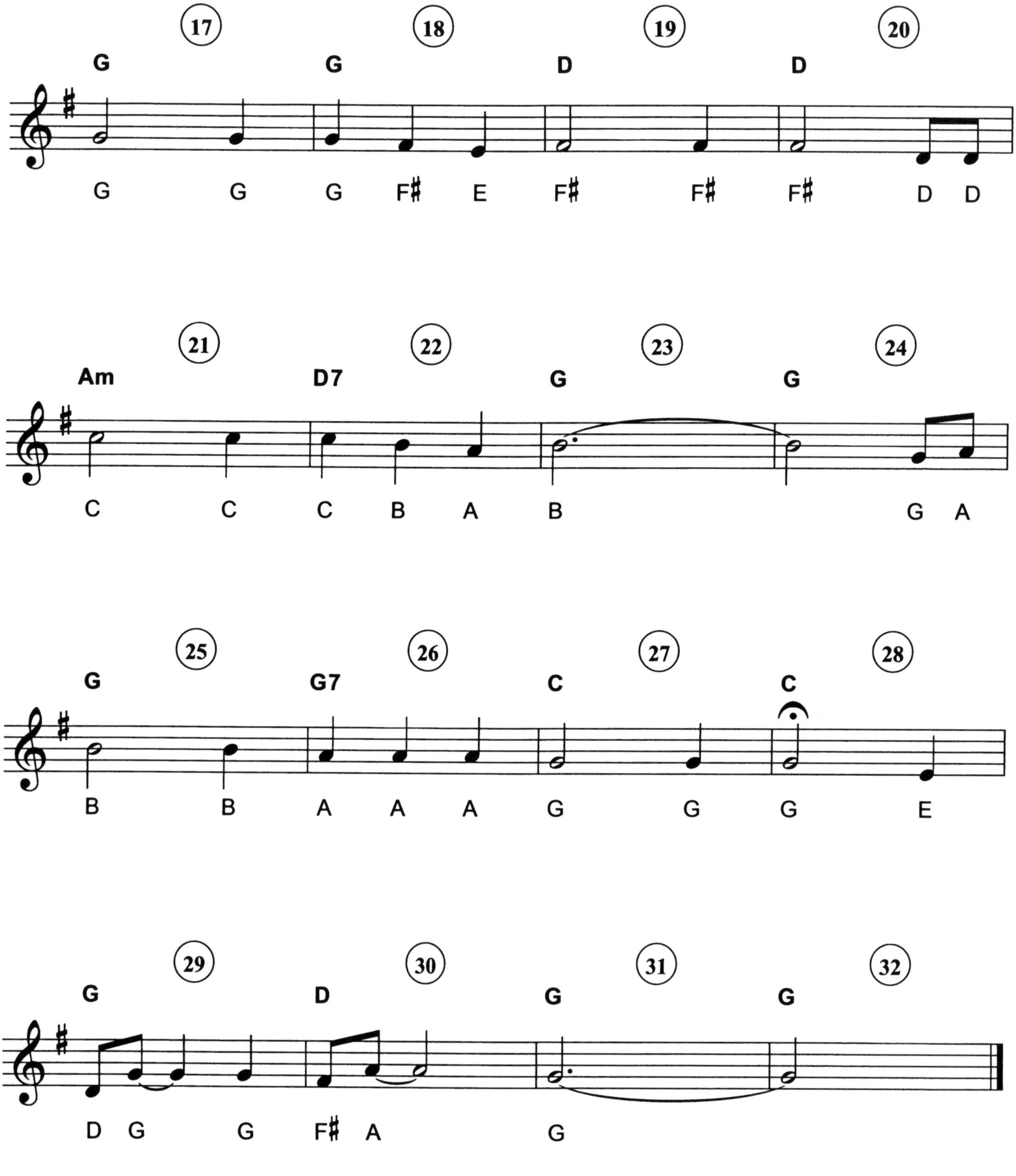

In the Garden

1 I come to the garden alone,
While the dew is still on the roses;
And the voice I hear, falling on my ear,
The Son of God discloses.

CHORUS: And He walks with me. and He talks with me,
And He tells me I am His own;
And the joy we share as we tarry there,
None other has ever known.

2 He speaks, and the sound of His voice
Is so sweet the birds hush their singing;
And the melody that He gave to me,
Within my heart is ringing.

CHORUS

3 I'd stay in the garden with Him,
Though the night around me be falling;
But He bids me go, thru' the voice of woe,
His voice to me is calling.

CHORUS

Silent Night

Key: C Major
Meter: Sets of 3

Joseph Mohr / Franz Gruber
Arranged by L.G.T.

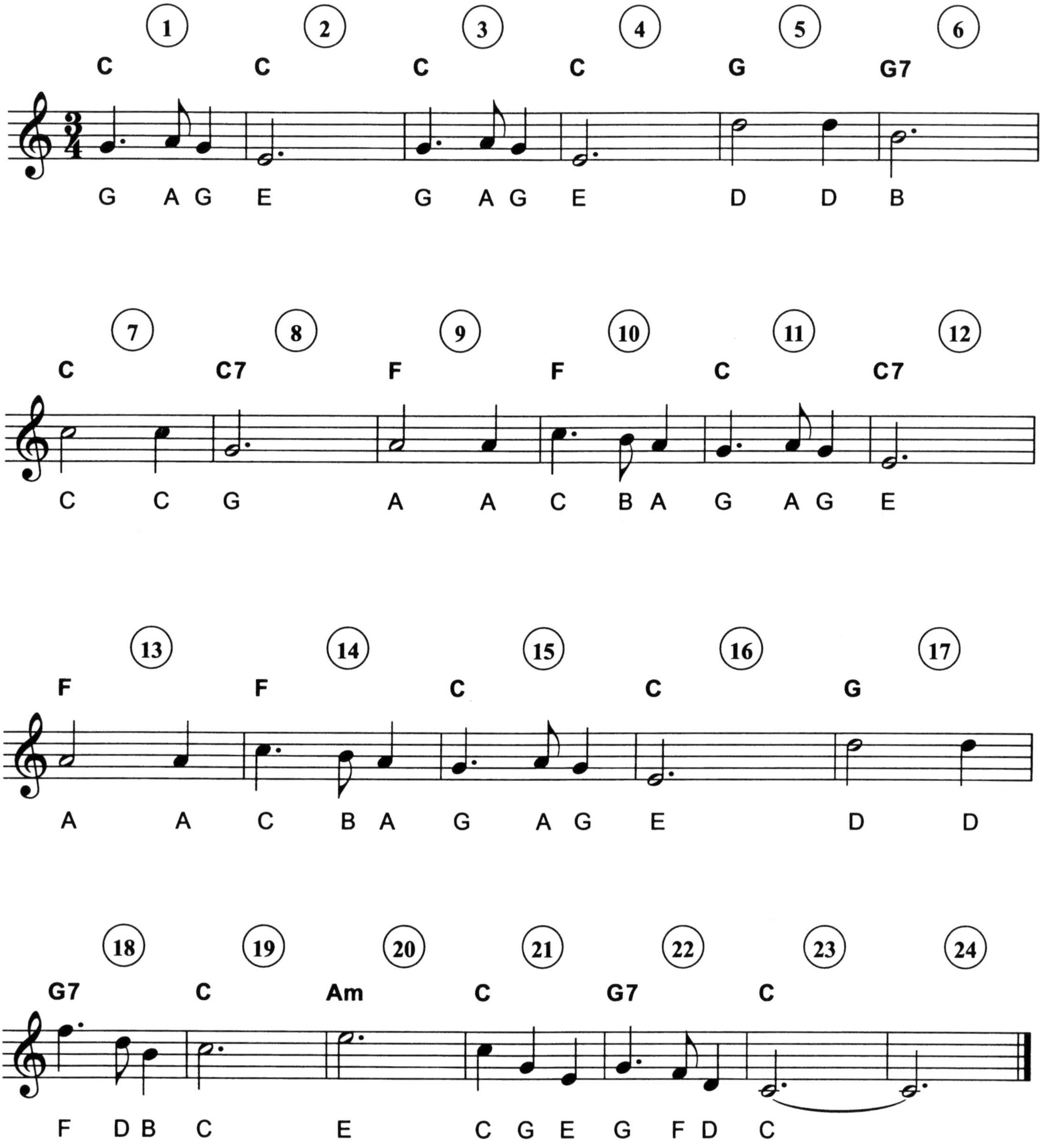

Silent Night

1 Silent night, holy night
All is calm, all is bright
'Round yon virgin mother and child!
Holy Infant, so tender and mild,
Sleep in heavenly peace, Sleep in heavenly peace.

2 Silent night, holy night
Shepherds quake at the sight,
Glories stream from heaven afar,
Heavenly hosts sing alleluia!
Christ, the Savior, is born, Christ, the Savior, is born!

3 Silent night, holy night
Son of God, love's pure light!
Radiant beams from Thy holy face
With the dawn of redeeming grace,
Jesus, Lord, at Thy birth, Jesus, Lord, at Thy birth.

St. Anne's Reel

Key: D Major
Meter: Sets of 4

Traditional
Arranged by L.G.T.

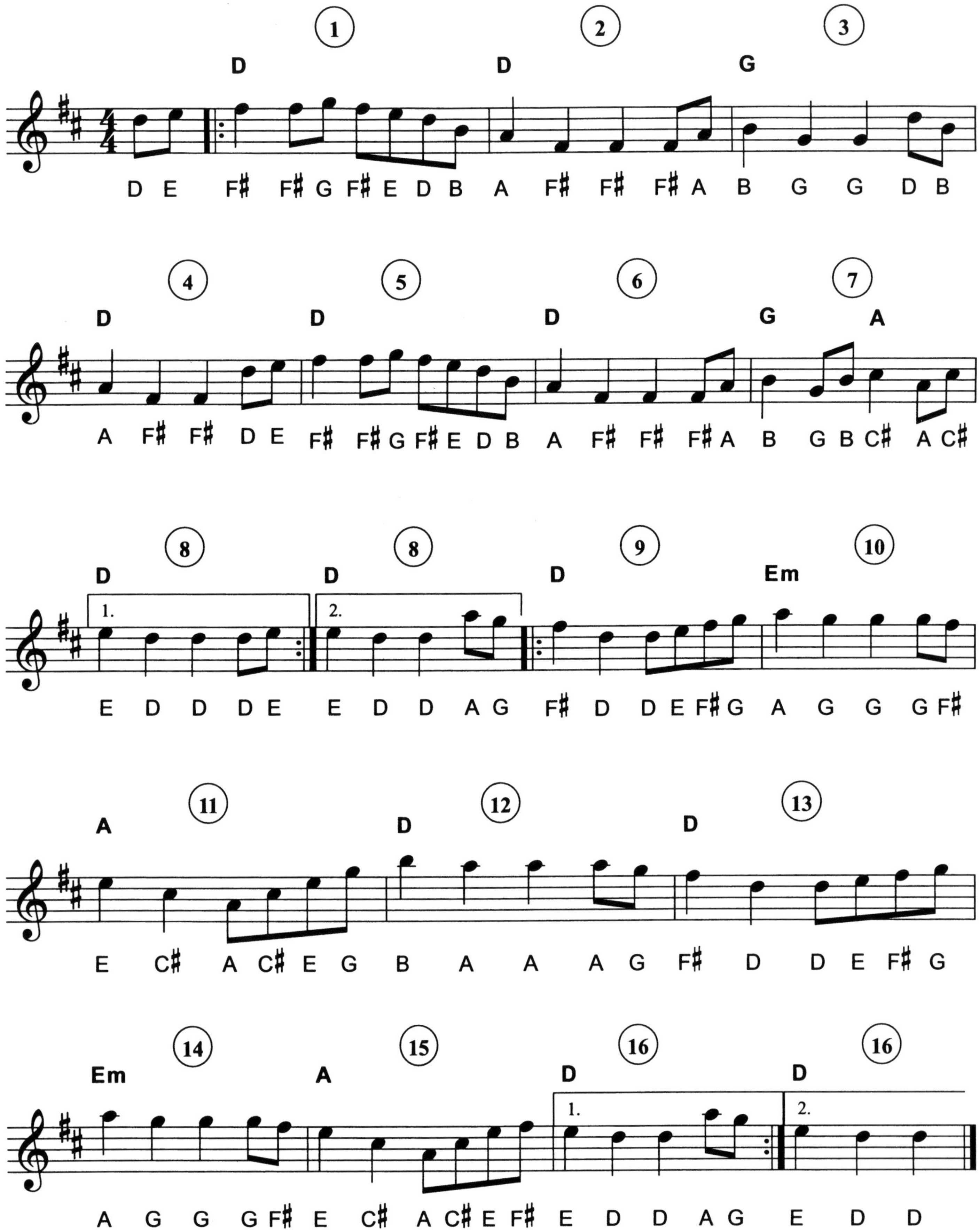

Sweet By and By

Key: G Major
Meter: Sets of 4

J.P. Webster
Arranged by L.G.T.

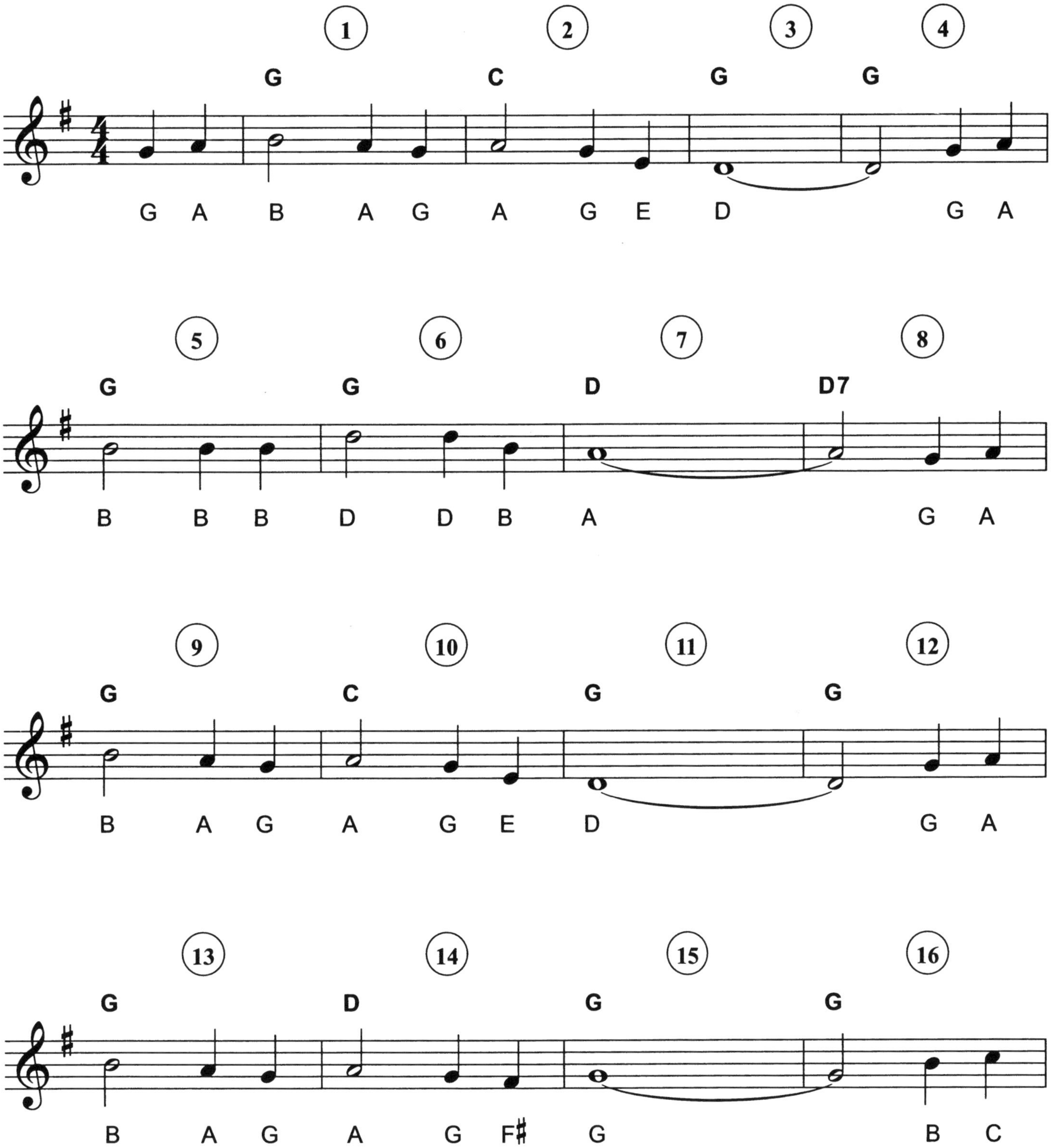

Continue

Sweet By and By (cont.)

CHORUS

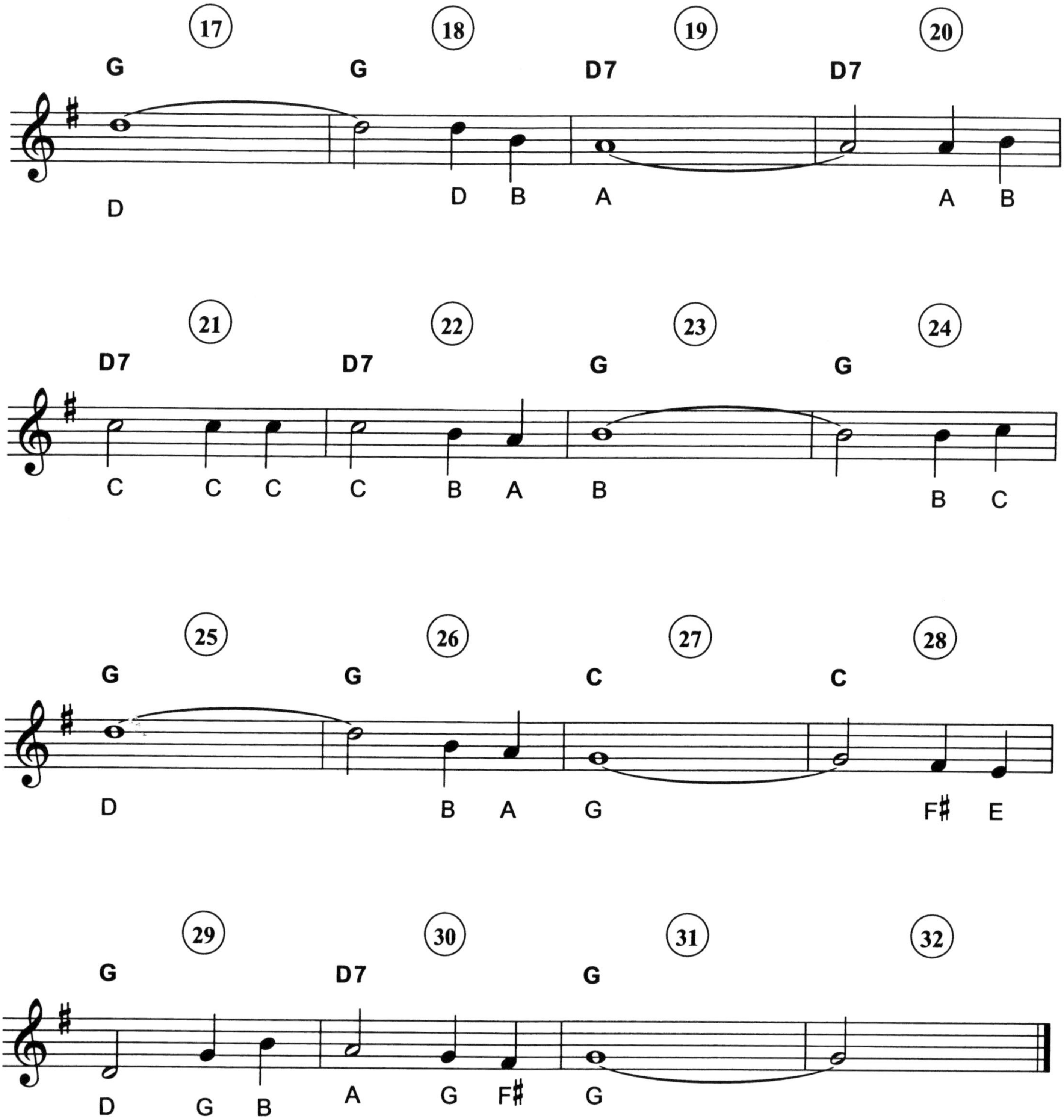

Sweet By and By

1 There's a land that is fairer than day,
And by faith we can see it afar;
For the Father waits over the way,
To prepare us a dwelling place there.

CHORUS: In the sweet by and by, We shall meet on that beautiful shore;
In the sweet by and by, We shall meet on that beautiful shore.

2 We shall sing on that beautiful shore,
The melodious songs of the blessed;
And our spirits shall sorrow no more,
Not a sigh for the blessing of rest.

CHORUS

3 To the bountiful Father above,
We will offer our tribute of praise;
For the glorious gift of His love,
And the blessings that hallow our days.

CHORUS

Sweet Hour of Prayer

Key: D Major
Meter: Sets of 3

Wm. B. Bradbury
Arranged by L.G.T.

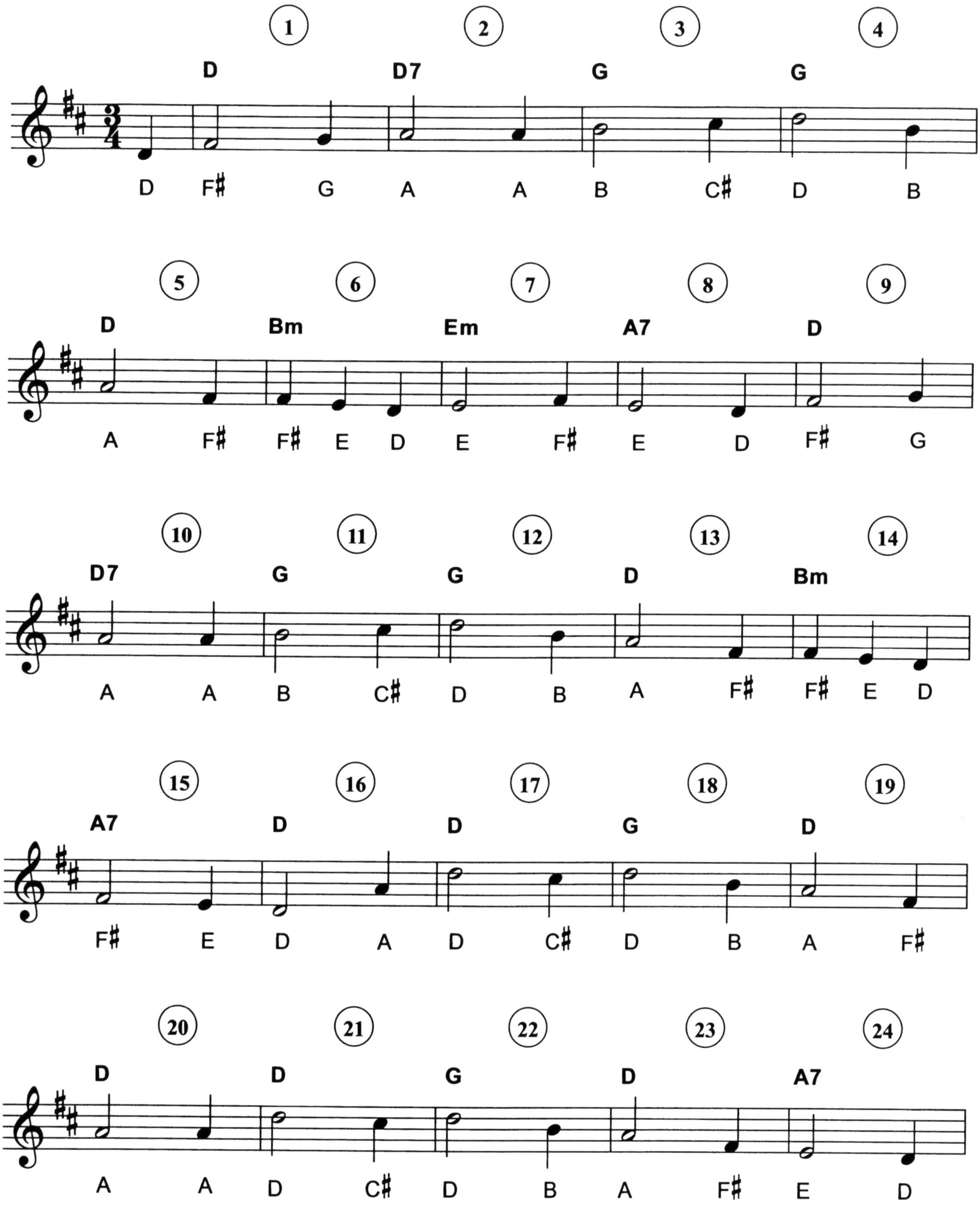

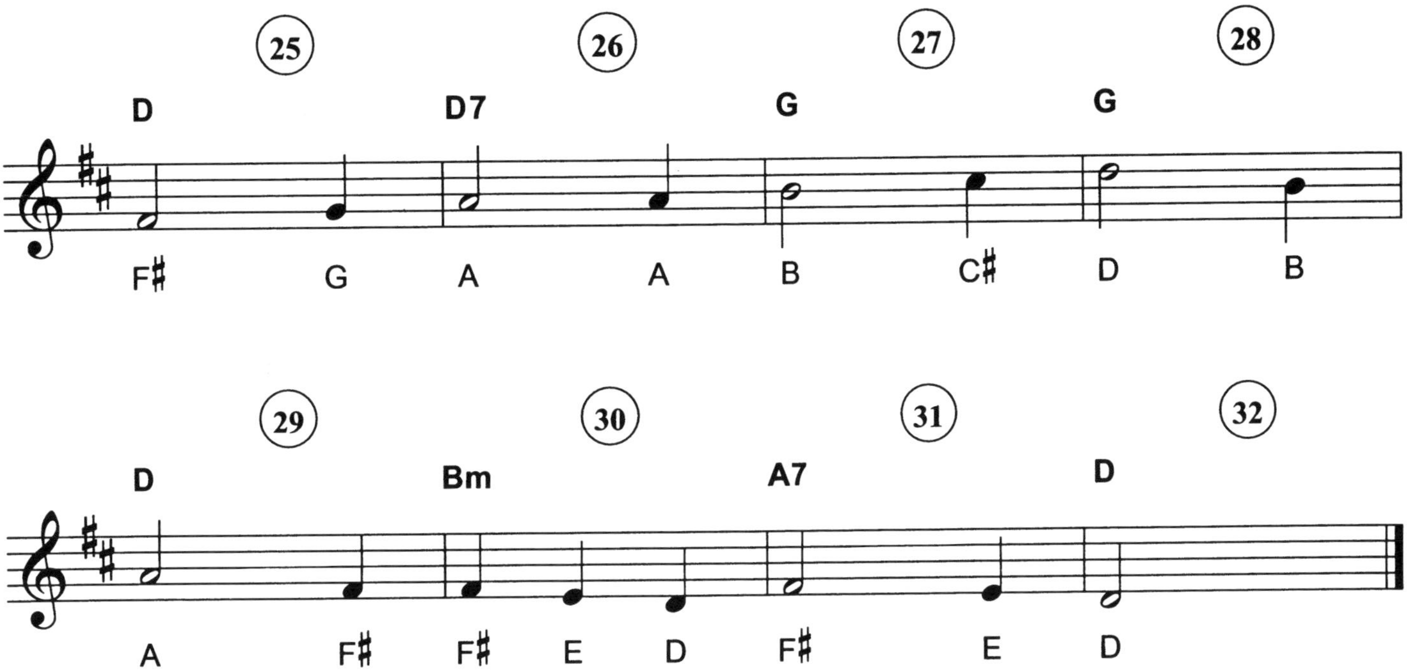

Sweet Hour of Prayer

1 Sweet hour of prayer! Sweet hour of prayer!
That calls me from a world of care,
And bids me at my Father's throne
Make all my wants and wishes known;
In seasons of distress and grief,
My soul has often found relief,
And oft escaped the tempter's snare
By thy return sweet hour of prayer.

2 Sweet hour of prayer! Sweet hour of prayer!
Thy wings shall my petition bear
To Him whose truth and faithfulness
Engage the waiting soul to bless;
And since He bids me seek His face,
Believe his Word and trust His Grace,
I'll cast on Him my every care,
And wait for thee, Sweet hour of prayer.

3 Sweet hour of prayer! Sweet hour of prayer!
May I thy consolation share,
'Til, from Mount Pisgah's lofty height,
I view my home, and take my flight:
This robe of flesh I'll drop, and rise
To seize the everlasting prize;
And shout, while passing through the air,
Farewell, farewell, sweet hour of prayer.

Linda Thomas's Discography

For Your Listening Pleasure

DL-OO1 PLAIN AND SIMPLE — A collection of fiddle tunes and waltzes featuring hammered dulcimer with acoustic guitar, mandolin, and bass. Titles include: *Ragtime Annie, Whiskey Before Breakfast, Liberty, Midnight On the Water, McKim's Reel, St. Anne's Reel, Willie's Waltz, Clarinet Polka* and more. AVAILABLE ON CASSETTE ONLY.

DL-002 MUSIC FROM THE HEART — A collection of fiddle tunes and waltzes featuring hammered dulcimer with acoustic guitar, mandolin, and bass. Titles include: *Rickett 's Hornpipe, Redwing, Jerusalem Ridge, Dulcimer Reel, Saturday Night Waltz, Cotton Patch Rag, Rosewood Casket, and Spinning Wheel* and more. AVAILABLE ON CASSETTE ONLY.

DL-003 MERRY CHRISTMAS — A collection of traditional holiday music featuring hammered dulcimer, acoustic guitar, mandolin, and bass. Titles include: *Joy to the World, It Came Upon a Midnight Clear, God Rest Ye Merry Gentlemen, Silent Night* and more. AVAILABLE ON CASSETTE ONLY.

DL-5/6 AMONG OLD FRIENDS — A compilation of PLAIN AND SIMPLE and MUSIC FROM THE HEART plus new titles: *Woodchopper's Reel, Cuckoo's Nest, Kentucky Waltz,* and *Flowers of Edinburgh* AVAILABLE ON CASSETTE AND CD.

DL-7/8 THE GATHERING PLACE — A collection of traditional hymns and gospel tunes featuring hammered dulcimer, acoustic guitar, mandolin, and bass. Titles include: *Pass Me Not, Mansion Over the Hilltop, Amazing Grace, How Great Thou Art* and more. AVAILABLE ON CASSETTE AND CD.

LGT-99 HOME — A collection of many new tunes featuring hammered dulcimer with acoustic guitar, mandolin, cello, flute, fiddle, accordion, bodhran, congas, and percussion. Titles include: *Bermudaful, Byrne's Hornpipe/Galway Hornpipe, Somewhere Along the Road, Ookpik Waltz, Cascade, For J.L., All About You, Greensleeves, Steamfolk Polkas, Squirrel On the Bed/Brecon Road, Azalea Waltz* and more. AVAILABLE ON CD ONLY.

LGT-OO AN OLD ENGLISH CHRISTMAS — A collection of 13th-16th Century carols featuring hammered dulcimer, acoustic guitar, mandolin, flute, recorder, cello and harpsichord. Titles include: *Children's Song of the Nativity, I Saw Three Ships, The Snow Lay On The Ground, The Friendly Beasts, The Golden Carol,* and more. AVAILABLE ON CD ONLY.

DDLT-1866 — A TURNING POINT — A vocal collection with accompaniments by hammered dulcimer, piano, acoustic guitar, mandolin, banjo, and bass. Titles include: *Home By the Sea, Little Green Valley, The Old Spinning Wheel, Lamp Lighting Time In The Valley* and more. AVAILABLE ON CD ONLY.

The above recordings are available direct from:
Linda G. Thomas
lindadan@primary.net
(816) 763-5040

Instructional Materials

PLAYING HAMMERED DULCIMER - A collection of hymns, folk songs, classics, holiday songs, and fiddle tunes aimed to help the less experienced player learn tunes on the hammered dulcimer quickly. This book comes with a companion recording, with great guitar accompaniment by Dan DeLancey, which provides ear training as a guide to learning the tunes. Dulcimer and guitar are conveniently recorded on separate tracks for independent practice with a rhythm track. The 33 titles include: *The Girl I Left Behind Me, Scarborough Fair, Aura Lee, St Anne's Reel, Pass Me Not, Old Joe Clark* and more. AVAILABLE IN STANDARD NOTATION WITH CD from Mel Bay Publications.

AN OLD ENGLISH CHRISTMAS - A collection of twenty 13th-16th Century carols arranged for beginner to the advanced player. The book includes tuning/explanatory charts, lyrics, and guitar chords, making the selections suitable for choir accompaniments! Titles include: *Children's Song of the Nativity, I Saw Three Ships, The Snow Lay On The Ground, The Friendly Beasts, The Golden Carol* and more. AVAILABLE IN STANDARD NOTATION WITH CD from Mel Bay Publications.

About the Author

Linda G. Thomas, a career music educator of 30 years, has performed on keyboard, guitar and hammered dulcimer for virtually her entire life. She was introduced to the music of the Ozark Mountains as a child and continued her studies to include B.S. in Education and Master of Arts in Teaching. Linda is a well-known performer in the circle of hammered dulcimer competitions having been a finalist in the Southern Regionals in 1994, '95, and '96. She was a finalist in the Texas State Championship in 1997 and 1998, and won that title in 1999.

Linda is receiving outstanding recognition for her instructional manuals for Mel Bay Publications as well as excellent reviews on her recording projects. She keeps an extensive performance and workshop touring agenda, maintains a private studio, and teaches public school music in Kansas City, Missouri. She, along with flat-pick guitarist Dan DeLancey, has been pleasing crowds throughout the United States and Europe and has become a much sought-after workshop presenter.

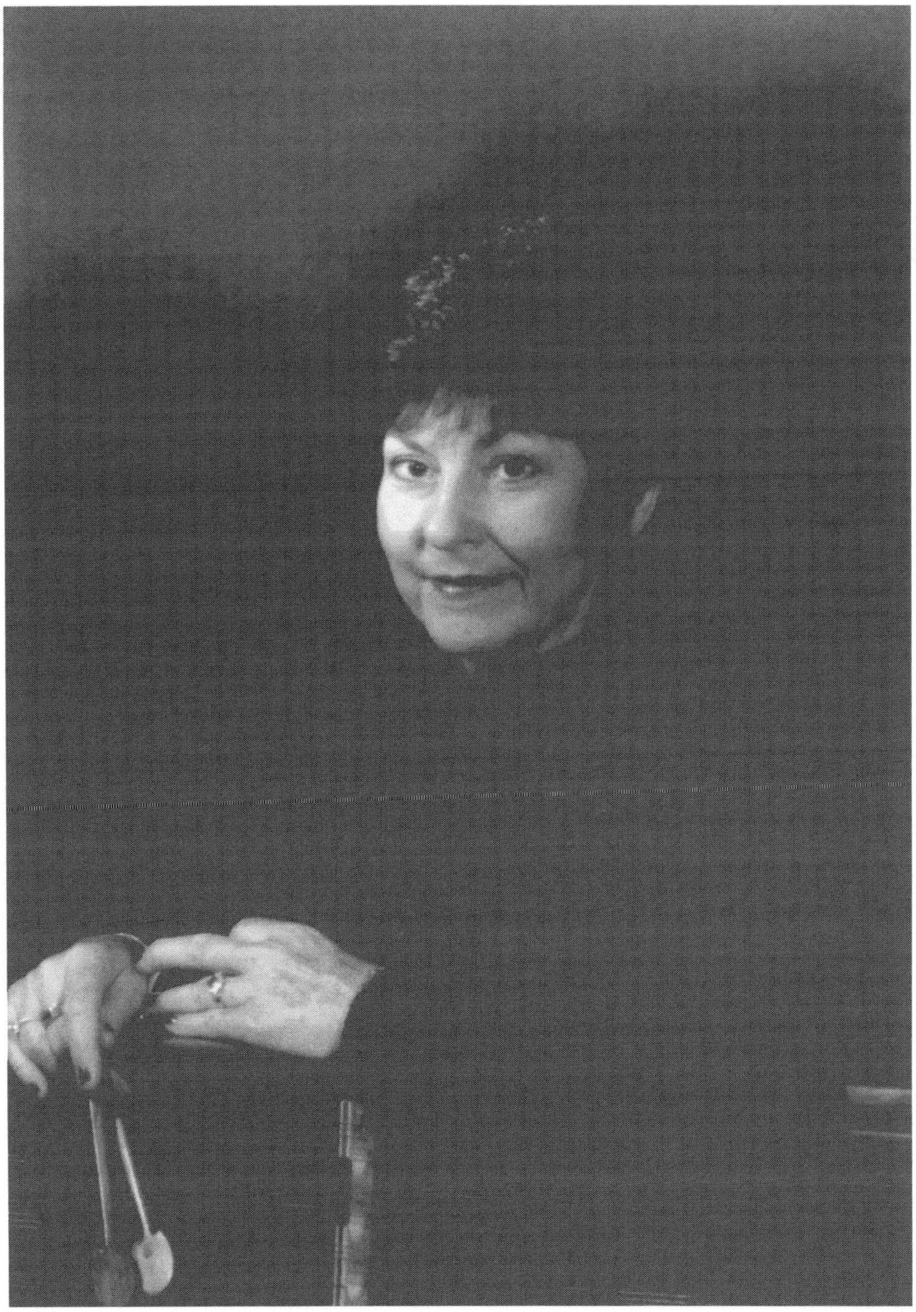

Linda G. Thomas

Selected Dulcimer Festivals and Workshops

Texas Dulcimer Festival, Glen Rose, TX.

Common Ground, Westminster, MD.

Great River Road Festival, Grafton, IL.

Ozark Mt. Folk Center, Mt. View, AR.

Kentucky Music Week, Bardstown, KY.

Buckeye Dulcimer Festival, Ashley, OH.

Steve Kaufman Acoustic Camp, Maryville, TN.

Central Mississippi Dulcimer Festival, Jackson, Miss

Clubs

The Focal Point, St. Louis, MO.

Sign of The Bear, Harwich, England

The Folk Club, Lowestoft, England

The Greyhound, Wivenhoe, England

The Woodshed, Carthage, MO.

Festival Concert Appearances

IBMA, Louisville, KY.

EWOB, Voortheisen, The Netherlands

Radio/TV Appearances

Public TV — Kansas City, MO.

Internet Broadcast —

Maryville, TN.

Louisville, KY.

Correspondence:
Linda G. Thomas
lindadan@primary.net
(816) 763-5040